DEFEAT AT
WATERLOO

Fighting on the Front Lines of the
Hillary Clinton Presidential Campaign

AMANDA WILKERSON

Published by amandawilkerson.org

Kissimmee, Florida

2011

ISBN-13: 978-1468141160
ISBN-10: 1468141163

Cover design by Killer Covers.

Printed in the U. S. A.

Pretty women wonder where my secret lies.
I'm not cute or built to suit a fashion model's size
But when I start to tell them,
They think I'm telling lies.
I say,
It's in the reach of my arms
The span of my hips,
The stride of my step,
The curl of my lips.
I'm a woman
Phenomenally.
Phenomenal woman,
That's me.---"From Phenomenal Woman"

by Maya Angelou

FOREWORD

I have had the pleasure of knowing Amanda Wilkerson for nearly a decade. Wilkerson was one of the founding members of the re-incorporated College Democrat chapters at Florida Agricultural and Mechanical University (FAMU). To put it simply, Amanda is lifelong, hard-charging politico committed to advancing progressive politics and empowering disenfranchised groups. She might have been born that way.

I met Amanda while matriculating at FAMU. She was not your typical co-ed. She was smart, articulate and fired up. She could trash talk and debate with the best of them. Her passion for politics and progressivism inspired me and legions of students to join the College Democrats, volunteer for local, state and national elections and advocate to human rights. But, there was more than meets the eye with this young lady.

Every family and individual has a story. With *Defeat at Waterloo: Fighting on the Front Lines*, Amanda challenges us to embrace our opportunity to latch onto the dreams that keep us awake in the middle of the night. Wilkerson's personal journey to Iowa and beyond is a metaphor for the distance between fear and faith. She takes us on a journey that explores how a determined spirit and winning attitude can transform ordinary creatures into people that perform extraordinary works.

There are very few moments that cause you to lose sleep. The winter of 2006 was filled with buzz about which Democrats might be running for President of the United States of America. Then came January 20, 2007 when Hillary Clinton announced on her website, "I'm In. And, I'm in to WIN." At that very moment, Amanda decided that she was all in, by any means necessary. That's when her mental wheels started churning and the universe began to help her beeline to Waterloo, Iowa as a Field Organizer for Hillary for President 2008.

Buckle up and enjoy the ride the story is extraordinary.

Zachary Rinkins,
Author of *It's PayDayBlog.com*

INTRODUCTION

*To my parents, sisters,
grandparents, aunts and uncles
and all of the wonderful mentors around
this country who provided me with wonderful
insight and meaningful guidance to help me
sustain in this struggle called life.*

*To any young man or women who have ever
tossed caution into the wind to run buck wild
after their dreams, even the unpredictable
political ones this book is for YOU!*

Z.R. I love you.

ACKNOWLEDGEMENTS

G rateful acknowledgment is extended to my wonderful parents, Dewey and Valerie Wilkerson for their loving support and awesome guidance. Dad you never did turn down an opportunity to give me your thoughtful feedback in the mist of what I thought was a big fiasco, not the campaign, but my life. Mom if God didn't make me divinely unique I would want to be a carbon copy of you. Help bring me down to earth when this ride is over.

Thanks to the following whose encouragement, guidance and mentoring help to shape this book:

Adeline L. Evans, Alexia Robinson, Amii McKendrick, Bernadette Morris, Christine Edel,

Cynthia Davis, Dawn Daise, Dewayne Harvey, Dewey and Louise Wilkerson Sr.,

Jonathan Kessler, Lindsey Eilon, Malcolm Glover, Melanie Maiden, Pamela Maiden, Paulette and Terrance Mitchell, Sonya Gardner, Zachary Rinkins.

I would also like to thank the production team at Create Space you guys were awesome and even though the process was new to me you made the experience wonderful. Killer Covers, lord I almost died when I saw the cover you produced. You guys are the best, go Emma go!To God be the Glory for all the wonderful things he has done!!!

INTRODUCTION

The words "community organizer" stand right next to the word "bitch" in my book. It's an overused phrase with little understanding of what it means, especially since so many people have derived at their own definition of the term. Ironically, you need look no further than the bitch who misunderstood the words to get my point. Some people like Sarah Palin think that community organizers have no responsibility and that our experiences don't prepare us to lead the world. Maybe not, but organizing, especially in the 2007 Iowa caucus, positioned me to gain skills that forced me to learn fast and lead so that my candidate could win. I am telling you this firsthand because on July 2, 2007, I boarded a Greyhound bus to do just that: ORGANIZE! I had the sheer pleasure and at times the excruciating pain to serve as community organizer for one of the most exciting presidential campaigns in years. The ups and downs of my work forced me to face a lot challenges that I had to skillfully maneuver myself through in order to position my team to accomplish the task we set out to meet. It certainly wasn't always easy but, in the end, I am everything I am today because of all that I went through.

The long rides up and down the cornfield-lined interstate of Iowa—a place that I had only read about but had hardly visited—truly tested my dedication to the process and the passion that brought me hundreds of miles away from the Deep South into modern-day Midwestern Iowa. I didn't realize then how prophetic that Greyhound ride was for me because the journey didn't end when the bus pulled into its final destination. The journey, in many ways, was just beginning. Throughout that expedition, I experienced many adventures; some were jarring and unusual, like the time one of the major black preachers openly pledged his support to the Clinton campaign. For me, it was a joyous occasion because it seemed that we were beginning to make some significant gains into the black community. To thank the pastor for his support, both Bill and Hillary Clinton joined him for a service, but no sooner had they left the corridors of the church building than he was directly quoted as saying he was an Obama supporter. Where was the loyalty?

Sometimes the adventure meant having to defend, time and time again, why this black girl, from the South no less, had decided to support a white woman over her own "kind": a black man. Many times the adventure was about seeing the campaign be out-organized by the Obama organization at almost all the major milestone caucus events.

For example, at the Harkin steak fry, our organization created makeshift instruments to drum up some support. Consequently, we were outdone when Obama came marching down to the entrance of the event with a real marching band, backed by the excitement of HUNDREDS of supporters following their "Drum Major for Change." The Clinton campaign truly made positive confessions that ignored the truth, in many respects, our organizational support was weak and, frankly, disorganized. All those adventures begin with the stories that you will read.

I must tell you that Hillary Clinton, in my mind's eye, remains the "Dean of Women" in politics. I know of no other individual who has such sustaining fortitude as she. So please note that this book is not to bash her at all. In fact, *Defeat at Waterloo* is a story that shares the memories of my work within the Iowa organization. Win, lose, or draw, these adventures were worth every bit of experience I gained. I hope you enjoy the ride as you share "my Greyhound ride to greatness" serving as a political operative in the Iowa caucus.

CHAPTER 1

BORN TO BATTLE

As long as I live, I will always remember the night I stepped into a middle-school gymnasium to participate in the grandeur of an event only political zealots can appreciate and understand: the Iowa caucus. As a South Floridian and Miami native, I had tortured myself for most of the Iowa winter by canvassing in the snow, attending round-table discussions, talking with local community stakeholders, pedaling supporter cards, dealing with rejection and unease only to face the reason I suffered through all of that discomfort in the first place: the Iowa caucus. Now I faced the daunting task of seeing the outcome of this work unfold into what I thought would be a wonderful evening of victory.

As I recall it, the buzz around our local campaign office made that day go by quickly, for I was sure that we would be on track to capturing the caucus. To be clear, it didn't matter that the track I was on meant that I was running in a circle, blind to the outside world that would have given insight into the disastrous night that I would face. You see, my life ran at a torpedo speed and I almost never had time to analyze outside predictions or projections; for me, it was work, hard work, and maybe a little sleep—and far too little of the last. And so what I faced that night can only be described as a horror story as the reality of the caucus results came rushing in. Truth be told, the people of Iowa had spoken and in the town where John Deere reigns supreme, the residents of Waterloo, Iowa, had successfully defeated the presidential aspirations of Hillary Clinton that night, and perhaps prophetically for that primary cycle. The domination of Obama'ss victory came across crystal-clear as I left the auditorium, racing to get back to the office to see how the result played out statewide. I don't know how I heard my cell phone ring as my thoughts raced loudly in my head; however, as I reached to pick up my phone, that one, single phone call cemented my worst fears about the crazy results. Stopping dead in my tracks, I heard the voice of a familiar sound. The news he gave confirmed what I saw in my caucus room about what happened all over the state of Iowa. In a brief phrase, it was all summed up: "Y'all lost."

It has taken me years to come to grips with the fact that my best efforts in organizing for whom I perceive as America's most unsung political heroine had ultimately lost the battle that essentially wrote the ending to her public career. I close my eyes now and all I can see are the hundreds of people who entered that auditorium on that bitter-cold Iowa night mostly all in support of Obama. As the people came in to the caucus, I was busy handing out processed cheese sandwiches to the handful of Hillary Clinton supporters who had gathered. The sight of all of the Obama supporters had me nervous and emotionally unwound. For heaven's sake, I was passing cheese as they chanted and cheered towards victory! Loads of pressure came crashing down over my exhausted body after I realized that the fight wasn't going to take all night, as I imagined. There would be no wheeling and dealing, no convincing people to cross lines and support my candidate. It wasn't a battle to the end, as I had played out in my mind. It would be—in fact, it was—quite the opposite: it was me going to a gun fight with a paper knife. The ammunition of the Obama campaign was new voters, which was the complete antithesis of the Clinton campain; we limited our reach to those true-blue caucus voters and that, my friends, made the big damn difference. To make matters worse, I walked head in hand, wondering if I was ever really ready to properly fight this battle.

Although that night I went back to the office to listen in on a conference call, I was numb to what had happened. My numbness drowned out my sensibilities and so I floated from one gathering to the next; finally, I ended up at a gathering for the black organizers of the HRC campaign in Waterloo. At the gathering, we shared a few stories of what happened in each of our caucus rooms but I was too mentally drained to sustain another round of "woe is me" get-togethers or unnecessary overindulgence of libation. Although I was dead tired, I went home and, in total silence, under the cover of darkness, pored over all of the emails I stored on my jump drive of how we were ahead. I read every piece of internal campaign memo that dictated where I needed to be in terms of hitting our number for that night. My heart skipped a beat when I saw how puny our numbers were when I considered the crowds of people Mr. Obama had organized. Hell, in the room I was in, all the campaign workers had predicted that, according to previous years' turnouts to the caucus, all we needed was fifteen people. We stood, shaky, in pale comparison to the never-ending stream of people that came for Obama. At one point I even checked outside to see if buses were dropping people off because, in my mind, I couldn't figure out how we could be so far behind and totally off base. There were no buses, though, just person after person filing into the auditorium of that school gym, and when they took their seats, they never got up, they never left; they sat and they were counted and, frankly, that's all that mattered.

I tried every now and then to call headquarters and alert them to the massacre that was occurring in my room but I was ashamed, not of me or my work, but of the outcome. When I sized up my competition in terms of strengths, there was no organizer who worked for Edwards or Obama who could hold a candle to the way I could move an audience with my words. I have presence, I am poised, and I'm a damn good organizer. Hell, I had organized at one of the largest historically black colleges in the nation: Florida A&M University. I was an active participant in student govern-ment, involved in the body of governance that allocates millions of dollars on behalf of its student constituents. I was the legendary director of student lobbying who secured relationships with elected political officials. In other words, I wasn't a novice to networking, organizing, or leading. I damn sure knew how to work a church; I grew up in one, and though it's hard to believe because of my potty mouth, my father is a pastor. But none of that seemed to work for me. I could sit and talk all day with leaders about supporting Hillary; many of them never said no to my invitation to speak or to my offer to join their support with mine, and some of them held out their support until the very end, but they wel-comed my enthusiasm. So why didn't it work? I do not really know but I'll share my stories and perhaps you can answer that question.

CHAPTER 2

THE GREYHOUND

My gateway Into the Corn Statelt was a sweltering hot morning in the early dog days of summer when I made the promise to myself not to allow another presidential campaign to roll by without being intimately involved—and I turned it into reality. I'd met the great Ann Lewis at a conference and expressed my interest in working for Hillary. Before long, I was offered an opportunity to go to New Hampshire or Iowa; luck would have it that I went to Iowa to sink my teeth into the political feast playing out there. I emptied out my bank account so that I could afford the Greyhound fare for my travel and, with nothing more than several dollars in my pocket and a dream, I gathered my belongings to make the long trip to Iowa to work on the Clinton exploratory campaign.

My expectations were set high. I believed that I would be able to say that I contributed to positioning Candidate Hillary Clinton to win the nomination and then to take the White House. I gathered my two suitcases, a footlocker, pillows, cover, and a fully charged cell phone and ventured into the makeshift lobby of the Tallahassee Greyhound station, which served as a gateway to my future. A quick nervousness ran through my body at the thought of leaving everything I knew to travel to a state hundreds of miles away. I gave Zach, my long-time live-in boyfriend, a quick peck on the cheek and never looked back because I was looking forward to the new adventure I signed up for.

As I sat in the seat, it dawned on me that I really didn't have the slightest idea as to how I was going to make things happen. A sense of panic abruptly hit me as I started thinking about the huge step I was taking, so to ease my nervousness, I wrote down all the things I wanted to do. I came up with one single goal—to win—and I carried that sheet wherever I went to remind me of my primary goal for coming to Iowa—not to make friends, not to enjoy the scenery, but to win. Wasting no time, I got on my laptop and tried to learn as much as I could about the great state of Iowa, and my research nearly scared me. Without knowing exactly where the campaign was planning to send me, one thing I learned that was crystal-clear was that they weren't many black people in Iowa. That wouldn't have made a whole heck of a difference except for the fact that I would be "housing" with a campaign supporter for the duration of the time that I was in Iowa. Frankly speaking, my name doesn't exactly give away my race or ethnicity, and I was nervous not so much for me but for the other person who would get a pleasant surprise when I rang their doorbell. I cringed. My whole bus trip was now filled with the anxiety over my living arrangements.

Guess Who's Home?

My first days on the campaign trail were fast and furious. I went to the headquarters of "Hillary Clinton for President" and was basically underwhelmed by the look of the office. Welcome to campaign world. People's belongings were nearly kept hidden on the surface of any desk space and everyone sort of worked on furniture that looked borrowed or stolen from a dump truck. The building was nice on the outside but inside, instead of a nice desk with leather swivel chairs, tables served as desks and chairs could be anything. My eyes quickly connected to a board filled with pictures or head shots of organizers who were scattered all across Iowa. Finally, a woman came to me and said, "You must be Amanda." It was Denise, the person in charge of field organizers for the Iowa operation. After exchanging less than a few words of causal greeting, we jumped in her car so that she could show me where I would be staying for the evening.

Luckily, I was relieved to find out that I would be staying at the house where local organizers lived. That feeling quickly left as Denise and I got lost; what made matters worse was that Denise got her car stuck in the yard of a complete stranger. I sat silently praying that this awkward moment would pass but things worsened and no one from the campaign could come to help. After very little contemplation, we were forced to knock on the door of the person's yard we were in. Trying to seize the moment, I put my best foot forward to show my boss that I was not afraid of introducing myself to new people, grabbed a piece of Hillary Clinton chum, and stepped up to the door. Before I could ring the doorbell, the porch lights came on and the one thing I was afraid of happening happened: the woman opened the door and her dog came running out. I am deathly afraid of dogs so I did the best thing I knew to do: run. This, of course, didn't help our efforts because the woman looked stunned as if I were participating in some sort of prank.

Denise quickly stepped in to explain the situation. Thank God Iowans are like Southerners when it comes to helping and being hospitable; they just don't turn down an opportunity to assist. She called her husband, who was just up the street. We knew he was arriving because he came barreling down the road in a pick-up that he and his buddies were in, and jumped out of the back of the truck to assess the situation. The man informed us that he would be able to help after he got his tools. So he went into the house and came out with cans of beer for him and his buddies. I thought to myself, *Welcome to Iowa*. We got out of that situation and even got a supporter card signed.

That night I slept tight because tomorrow I would be going to Waterloo, Iowa, the new city I was assigned to organize in to participate in the Fourth of July events scheduled for the campaign trail. Still with no clue as to where I would be living, I slept soundly and was ready for a new day. The morning came sooner than I expected but I was glad to see it. I showered, got dressed, and waited outside with all of my meager belongings for the next destination: Waterloo. When my ride arrived, we set out on a journey more than two hours away from Des Moines, Iowa.

As we rolled down the interstate, I was curious about all of the beautiful farms we saw along the way and the fields upon fields of corn that we passed. I was snapped out of my pre-comatose daze to find myself in Waterloo. I got out of the car to find out that I was overdressed for an event that would take place outside. Although I was introduced to the regional field director, everything he said washed over me since everyone was moving at a hundred miles per hour as they prepared for Hillary Clinton and President Clinton to do their first joint campaign push together. Finally, he stopped, looked at me, and said, "Get to the gates. I'll introduce the gang later." That promise was short-lived when I met the first person that I would be sharing an office with. He mistook me for a volunteer and barked several orders at me. It was funny to see him in action; he was an intense white boy named Ben and, to be honest, he was one of the hardest-working, fiercely passionate organizers that I had the pleasure of meeting. Because I wanted to survey who had the power and how all of my new co-workers operated, I didn't immediately mention who I was. The event gates opened and people poured in. Standing there, I couldn't help but think, *Well, where are the black folks?* At the end of the day, I think I could count them all on my hand, and Waterloo was supposed to be the city that had the highest concentration of African-Americans in the state.

The event ended and I was introduced again to Jamaal, a young black man who was the regional field director. He told me to jump in his car and my anxiety level gradually rose because I thought we were going to my new home. But we just got on the road to go to the next location. This was my first realization on the campaign trail that the work of an organizer literally never stops. I think that's the edge, though, that makes the work fun.

As we drove, he didn't say much because he was on and off every conference call imaginable. As soon as we pulled into the town we were supposed to be in, he stopped at a hotel, put me there for the night, and told me that everything we did today we would do tomorrow so "get sleep and get up early." By "early," I believe that man meant the crack of dawn because when he rung my room and couldn't wake me and then knocked on the door at five-something in the morning, I nearly died because I wasn't ready. Though the day started off rocky, we duplicated everything we did the day before once again at this event, even down to "jump in the car...we're going to the next city." Unlike yesterday, the next city was back to Waterloo.

I may have spent a few days with a co-worker in his cramped basement apartment, which he graciously shared with me, but after that my supporter housing was secured and I was off to face my nightmare. Andrew, my young co-worker, drove his car in front of the house where I would be staying. It was stunningly gorgeous. He walked to the door with a portion of my belongings and an older white woman approached the door: Val. I walked in and she asked, "Well, where is Amanda?" In my mind, I thought, *Oh, shit, here it goes*. Before Andrew could say a word, I stepped forward and introduced myself as Amanda Wilkerson, her new roommate. It didn't take long for her to show her uneasiness. Although she was kind, I could tell that she was jarred. I didn't want Andrew to leave but I knew he didn't want to stay. Val didn't want Andrew to leave so she kept asking a million and one questions on where Candidate Clinton stood on a number of different areas. Finally, after several moments of awkward silence, Val looked over at me and said, "So when do you think you are leaving?" I was horrified. What the heck did she mean? The campaign promised me that I would have supporter housing to defray the cost of coming to work on the campaign, and yet, in my mind, she was already kicking me out.

Andrew slipped out during this time so, without knowing exactly what to do, I just started talking. Hell, it didn't particularly matter to her that I was black; what mattered was that I was a stranger in her house. I tried to talk to her and share a little bit about myself to put her at ease and that did the trick. I loved living with Val; it actually was one of the most rewarding aspects of living in Iowa. She genuinely grew to care for me and this made sense because July to January is a long time and if we were going to spend it together, we had to like each other. I couldn't go home for Thanksgiving or Christmas; however, she made both of my favorite holidays cherished ones. She would even assure my parents that she was taking good care of me.

She was a Hillary Clinton supporter and she didn't take no mess from anybody that came to her house to talk about their candidate. She would let them know in a Miami minute that "this is a Hillary house and I have a Hillary Clinton big-time worker living with me, so that's where my support is." I laugh thinking about all the nights she would stop me from going to bed just to quiz me about what I had done that day. When I needed help trying to locate different key people in the black community, I would rely on her because she knew them all as a long-time realtor and active Democrat. I relied on her insight as a navigational tool to help me during my time organizing in Iowa. She supported me beyond just having a place to stay. Val, a more than eighty–year-old woman, was a friend.

An organizer must never forget that fear is an emotion that can be fatal to your assignment. Walk into a situation prepared and dictate the terms when it comes to how each interaction with the public will get you closer to your goals. Anxiety stops action; fear is fatal and anxiety is awkward. Make your first impression—your first move—your best move, but no move can be made without preparation. A mindless move is a dangerous one. So move with purpose and on purpose.

CHAPTER 3

ORGANIZING WOES OF WATERLOO

Organizing can be a difficult thing because you can trust no one outside the campaign and sometimes in the campaign; you can only trust your instinct. There were days when I practiced this thought with ease and little effort; other times I had to masterfully come up with plans of action on how I would treat small situations. Even though they were small, the emotions could be huge. Now that I was in the office working full-time, I was very careful of how I would manage dealing with the idiosyncrasies of organizing and, to tell you the truth, one can get her panties in a bunch figuring this one out.

Settling in was taking effect and now the real politics began to take place. There was another black organizer, Doris, who worked for the campaign in Waterloo. She was in her mid-thirties and had grown up in the city of Waterloo. She had children and was the oldest staff member in our office. Everyone else was just out of college with no kids. I suppose that her direct responsibility was to gather support for Hillary Clinton among the people she grew up with— except it was always hard to trust what she was doing because she rarely ever shared information that was con- crete enough to show she was making any gains. I decided that I was going to keep my distance so that I could learn a little bit more about her before I leaped in. This didn't work because her puzzlement about my being there meant her bull's eye was directly on me. Eventually she invited me to have lunch with her and I knew accepting the invitation meant I was going to get more than a blue-plate special at the local eatery.

Once we met, she casually made it clear to me that none of the black people in the community knew me and that raised their suspicions about me. Bullshit! They proba- bly didn't know the dean organizer or any other organizer, for that matter. Why would it matter that they didn't know me? This all ran through my head but what came out of my mouth was, "This is why we should work together...so you can introduce me. That way, I could get to know the community." Feeling like I was already wasting my time, I was ready to end the conversation and at least enjoy the meal I ordered because I knew that this wasn't going any-where. She continued to drop subtle hints that I wasn't ideal for organizing an area she grew up in. Then she asked me a question that put the entire conversation in perspective. Let me say that while we worked in the office together, she almost never said anything to me—at ALL! So the fact that she was willing to talk to me now puzzled me, but her con-versation was putting the picture together for me, espe-cially when she asked why the campaign had brought me there. I took my time answering this because at no point had anyone mentioned to me, a fairly new organizer, that I was there to take over someone's place, and from what I could gather, campaigns or any good organizations never talk about HR information with other employees, so what-ever secret there was about her job was not made avail-able to me. Plus, it was never my intention to talk about our jobs; I was not there to take her job. I listened for as much as I could take then finally stopped her and said the magic words that eased her fears and my agony: "What can I do to help?"

We negotiated working with each other and sketched out who we would talk to. Sounded easy enough until she started listing key people that she considered to be arch-enemies—for example, State Representative Berry or the wife of black public radio station owner Louise Porter. I mean, the list of people that she could manage to talk to was shorter than the list of people that she really couldn't deal with. What was important to me was that one way or another we touched base with people in the community to get the word out that Candidate Clinton was a leader whom they could count on to accomplish goals that would directly impact their community, from Washington, D.C. all the way to Waterloo. If that meant talking to the people she had no interest in working with, I was fine with that. We had a clear understanding and that's what really mattered. The meeting was over and it was time to manage our agreement—and this was all in a week's work. So after we ended our discussion, the campaign abruptly ended her tenure with the organization. It was a simple call that ended everything and instead of feeling pity for her, I quickly used the opportunity to capture the territory she controlled and place it under my organizational management. However, I forgot one of life's golden rules, which is "first impressions are lasting ones." Her abrupt dismissal from the campaign turned out to be a major curse before I could ever see it as a blessing.

I never questioned the campaign, though; not only was it not my place to do so, but my pride prevented me from

asking about a predecessor when I now had the opportunity to make my mark. It was my turn and I wanted to
turn things around for the good. But folks in the black community didn't see it like that. In fact, the many calls that
I made to see or speak with people were never returned
until word got around that Doris was off of the campaigning. Now my phone was ringing day and night and I was
setting up go-sees and one-on-ones with stakeholders
that were significant in the African-American community.
My first meeting with was with a woman who was the disc
jockey for the local black radio station on Sundays. She had
a warm smile and a big personality; when Joyce spoke, she
exuded excitement...until I told her that Doris was gone.
This was right after she asked me where Doris was since she
had come to the office specifically to see her. I tried breaking the news like I always did: hell if I knew where she was,
but Candidate Clinton is running for office and I needed
to re-direct the conversation back to her. I asked Joyce
what she thought about Hillary Clinton instead of directly
answering her question about Doris. Wrong move! She shot
me a look that could kill and I knew that whatever she was
about to say, I was going to get it. She point-blank asked
me without hesitation, "Does Hillary Clinton believe in lay-
ing off black single-with-children women who are the head
of their house? Because, if she does, I don't want to support her." I tried to remind her that if Doris was gone, the

campaign would not discuss the reasons for why she was no longer there. Joyce could have cared less; my smooth talking didn't do shit to change the fact that she felt as though I totally evaded her question. She basically walked out the door and I followed her; she said that since Hillary Clinton didn't support hard-working single women like Doris, she wanted me to think about what I was asking. I totally stuck my foot in my mouth…and with the wrong person at that! No matter what my intentions were, I didn't convince her about Hillary, nor did I answer her question, so now I was nothing more than a fast-talking black girl who did the bidding of a white woman who didn't care about Joyce or her community.

Sometimes you have to think fast on your feet instead of looking for all the eloquent words to say or apologizing insincerely. I immediately called Joyce and asked her to come back. As I waited for her to come, I drew a blank. I promised her that I would try to explain to the best of my ability and knowledge what I knew about Doris when, in reality, I could piecemeal a story together, but I would never be able to tell the truth because it wasn't at my disposal. Now I was angry. Why should I have to bend over backwards to explain this dilemma? Why did I have to even answer her question with my smart-ass remark?

No sooner had I started my self- depreciation than she came rolling back into the parking lot with a smile, no less, which put me off. Not because I don't like being greeted with a smile but because of the fact that she was smiling at all. What she said to me after she rolled down her windows explained her frustration: "Listen, girl, I know you are not from here and I know Hillary Clinton cares about people and women and black folks. It's just that everybody in the community is wondering why Doris is gone and now you are here." I hid my outrage with a blank stare; she may have thought that I was lost, but inside I was infuriated. Who was "everybody"? The bodies of people that, when I called, didn't return a call? The bodies of people that never met me but, because of Doris, had already formed an opinion about me? I couldn't help that people were suspicious about the campaign due to the fact that Doris was gone, but what in the hell did that have to do with issues like whether or not someone should have access to universal health care? The point being that I didn't come to Waterloo to have an all-out war, fighting over personal hang-ups. I came to win a political race.

She continued talking but all I kept thinking about was when I would begin to work on what I came there for instead of cleaning up drama I didn't create that had nothing to do with my candidate. She spoke and I listened, and the message was loud and clear: *you've allowed this to be a distraction and you have to get things on track; let her know that while you understand her point, you are there for*

Hillary Clinton. She stopped talking and before I could say anything, she said this: "I like you. It's something different about you. Don't stop what you're doing and I'll help you because I'm not committed to anybody right now. So just call me." This started a series of the woes that I would face as I tried to successfully organize my precincts.

The fact of the matter is you can't avoid chaos like that; you have to learn how to work through it without being stuck in it…and I had to learn, sometimes the hard way, to respond but never react to a situation. My response was to call her back to clear the air; a reaction could have been to plead my case, let her know that I was altogether sick of this crap, and if we couldn't talk about the caucus or Clinton then our conversation would be limited. The fact of the matter is, as an organizer, I manage the image of my candidate on the front line, and this type of reaction would have severely impacted her integrity in my community despite who was right or wrong or who was at fault. Eventually, the lesson was learned but those experiences never stopped because that is what organizing is all about.

With no help and very limited insight into the structure of how the community operated, I was virtually on my own and I had to start connecting with people to at least see where they stood on supporting Hillary. Where were the people with the power?

I came home one night drained because I had yet to find the answer to that troubling question. As I walked into the house, Val greeted me as she always did from her bedroom with the door ajar. She would beckon me to come into her room. I usually would consent to doing so because talking to her was my way of venting, but lately I had begun to do it out of duty, agreeing to speak even if I just wanted to go to bed. We chatted for a while and I guess she sensed that something was troubling me. Normally when she felt that way, she would just let me go to bed and maybe we would continue the conversation over breakfast, as we usually did, but that wasn't her remedy for that night. "What's eating you up? You only answer the questions I ask. It's like talking to a questionnaire," she said.

I didn't know how candid I could be with Val because I only like to expose problems if I feel like the person can help me find a solution. At first, I hesitated to answer her question but she knew I was bullshitting so she pressed me until I told her the truth. "Val, I really don't know how to get in touch with leaders of the black community on the east side of Waterloo. It doesn't matter that I call nightly hundreds of homes. Somehow, people weren't home. Or they would pick up the phone and tell me that this was all starting too early for them and because I called on behalf of my candidate, they were no longer considering supporting her. It's becoming a delicate lineof trying to figure out if I should push a little or try back."

I explained this all to Val and she sat quietly and listened. When I noticed that I had been talking on and on about why I was so upset, I stopped. In my head, I wanted to say, "What the hell can you do to help me? You live on the west side of Waterloo. The closest you come to the east side is to visit the campaign office, which is really downtown Waterloo, which divides both the east and west side." What she managed to say after I went on a five-minute tirade almost made we want to step back on my soap box of self-pity: "Get some sleep. It will be better in the morning."

I jumped the hell up out of her room and kept thinking to myself, *Don't react; just respond.* My response was crying myself to sleep. What in the hell was I going to do? I woke up the next morning and Val had breakfast made and a cup of coffee waiting forme. I came into the kitchen and decided that I would go into work early to try to sort things out without the noise of the office or dealing with Val. Good luck with that because when Val said, "Sit down and have a cup of coffee," I couldn't turn her down. As I slowly sipped my coffee, she asked, "Did I hear you crying last night?" Damn, that was embarrassing; she heard me at my most vulnerable moment. Was I supposed to tell her no? "Yeah, Val, I'll try to keep it down next time."

"You know what, Amanda? You can't cry; you have to fight. You have to dig; you have to keep your goal in mind." I heard all of this before so I tried not to get aggravated at hearing the same message twice. She handed me a slip of paper and said, "These are all the people that you need to acquaint yourself with on the east side of Waterloo. I've worked with them all on different social action committees and when you talk to them, tell them that Val Martin told you to get in touch with them. Willie Mae Wright's daughter died not too long ago, so don't call her. Go see her but don't talk politics. Tell her who you are and why you are there, but she needs love. Talk with Anna Mae Weems; she's done so much with civil rights in this town and when she speaks, she gets the attention of a lot of people. She's a tough cookie but she'll let you lay out your case for supporting Hillary. Go to BJ Furgerson; let her talk to you about the history of Eastside Waterloo and then tell her that she can make history again with Hillary."

Oh, the list included the information I needed and with Val's background on each individual, I had the knowledge on how I should address them. Then Val took me to about four houses that she owned over in the area and said I could put yard signs in the ones that weren't occupied. This was all very overwhelming; it was my prayers answered and I couldn't thank Val enough. I concluded that morning's conversation with at least seventeen different points of contacts. The tears quickly dried; she gave me the life-lines I needed and I used them to talk to these women and introduce myself.

It was a pleasure meeting these women, but from the moment I spoke with them, I could see in their eyes that persuading them to support Clinton would be a feat. You see, many of them were well into their seventies and the thought of supporting the first possible black president was far more exhilarating. But many of them took me under their arms and would let me talk my talk because at the very least they supported me. Whether it was a home-cooked meal or valuable information, all I had to do was stay in touch and somehow they would reach out and touch me. This opened many doors for me to get in touch with preachers because instead of cold-calling, I was being referred by these ladies to go and speak with their lay ministers. Again, things picked up for me and I was now experiencing exciting times in organizing.

I had made contact with elected officials. That was easy—they had to make themselves available; that's the nature of the game: the community movers and shakers and now on to the preachers. Talk about long-winded conversations about nothing! At least when I walked in the door, they knew I had an agenda. I was the one blind-sided; I had no idea that they would have agendas!

Traditionally, I felt like the only reasons campaigns went to the black churches were because they served as the equalizing force in the black community and were used as a way to rally the parishioners for social change, like Dr. Martin Luther King or Rev. Jesse Jackson did, or even to a lesser extent Rev. Al Sharpton. Some would request funding for their pet projects and downright ask if they could get any money to support my candidate. Clearly, they neglected to realize that this was a political campaign and not a Ponzi scheme. I didn't mind them asking; as long as I had an invitation to come and speak, I was A-okay. Sometimes the conversations went well; for instance, I had the opportunity of meeting a female pastor whose name was Belinda. I don't recall her last name but she made a lasting impression on me because, out of all the ministers I talked to on the Eastside of Waterloo, she was among the ones that represented the purpose of Christ well.

I came to her office and I laid on thick that I wanted her support and I needed her to commit. I listed all my reasons for why this woman should support Hillary and even gave her my reasons for coming all the way to Iowa to work for my candidate. After I was done, she looked me squarely in the eyes and told me that she agreed with all of the information that I had given her and was honest enough to let me know that while she had not committed one way or the other, publically she felt that it was only right to tell me that she knew in her heart that she was going to the caucus for Obama. Normally when someone told me that they weren't supporting Hillary, I got mad internally. I was saddened by her choice but at least I didn't go on a wild goose chase to get the truth.

There were other pastors and lay minsters that loved Hillary. Rev. Logans and his wife were an example of that. It didn't take long for them to commit and, when they did, they were outspoken supporters of the candidate and our organization, fighting supportively. Then there were pastors who talked a good game and played games; an example of that was Franz Whitfield of Mount Carmel Baptist Church, right there on the Eastside of Waterloo. I would go and talk with him from time to time to keep him plugged in about Candidate Clinton and to encourage him to support her. His interest in Clinton was so very important to the campaign that the Iowa operation employed the resources of the national organization, utilizing the African-American Outreach to open up more support for Hillary Clinton among the pastor community. The leaders who came from D.C. to help with this effort weren't novices when it came to doing this sort of outreach; in fact, they had done it before for candidates like Clinton and I was thrilled to see them arrive. Together, we collaborated, taking what I was already doing to get access to the preachers. And then the news came down the pipe that a local young pastor of one of the most premiere congregations was starting to break our way for Hillary.

Frantz Whitfield was a Clinton supporter, and to personally thank him for his support, not only was Hillary Clinton going to attend church service but one of the baddest Southern Baptists this side of heaven would accompany her as well: her very own husband, President Bill Clinton. Word spread rather quickly in the community and to celebrate this homecoming of sorts, the church worked with the campaign to put on a dinner after the service for key community activists. The day arrived for the Clintons to attend Mount Carmel and I had an icky feeling about everything. One of my supporters tipped me off that she thought that Whitfield had already committed his support for Obama. I drummed up her inconvenient bad news as being her way of showing me her disgust that she was not invited to the dinner reception after the service. Then when I walked in through the church doors, there was a huge Obama box with buttons on the table and bumper stickers! Because, at that point, I was the only one in that area of the church, I stuck this box right under the table.

Things only grew stranger from there when the Clintons arrived. People were excited and when it was time to pass the peace, folks came up to the Clintons to give hugs and take pictures. Being a preacher's kid, I knew this presented a problem because this is a huge taboo in the black church; it's a place of worship, not for paparazzi seeking photo ops. The people taking the pictures were obviously not members.

Church went as normal but it just never felt right. The only thing that I considered to be extremely genuine was when President Clinton took off his power tie and gave it to Frantz. I was glad when that day was over and I was glad that it seemed that we had gotten the support of a major minister—except, according to an article I read on NewYorkTimes.com, the right reverend himself was not actually in support of Hillary Clinton at all. In his mind, he had an obligation to support Obama because of the old folks. What a crock of pure, indigestible shit!

Listen: caucusing is a choice, and once someone firmly told me who they were supporting, I marked it off in my book that I kept and then continued contact in hopes that I could at least create doubt in their minds. On the other hand, when I got a supporter to supporter Hillary, I would do my best to invite them to all our events, which meant exposing them to other supporters.

As I read the article, tears ran slowly down my cheeks; even if he had signed a supporter card for Hillary Clinton—which he did—and was no longer in support of her, it would have been nice not to read it on the front page of a news organization website. I don't even know if he thought about anyone other than himself as he processed through his indecision. Of course, his choice is his choice, but his choice could have affected the livelihood of people working on the campaign. I'm not sure what his explanation was because, at the end of the day, no reporter can misquote your actions. I was done with preachers; sure, they open their doors and meet with us, but the people they were leading weren't open to us. And the whole Frantz Whitfield debacle made the campaign look out of touch with the community we were organizing. I wanted to step up my efforts and talk directly to the people without using the phones or our events, since most times I rarely got an answer or I hardly saw them at our event.

I lived in Waterloo for a while now and because I worked weird hours, I didn't know where people met for coffee or where they took their kids for a nice time. Where did they meet for NAACP meetings or other community-related events? I wandered in several different places to find these common folk and the unexpected happen. At a Democratic event, I was introduced to a local college professor named Dr. Micheal Blackwell. When I introduced myself and told him that I was from Florida and had attended Florida A&M University, he kept asking me if I knew a girl named Maria. I racked my mind to figure out who he was talking about but I always drew a blank. In fact, he wasn't the only person to ask me about this Maria. He and others figured that I must have known her since both she and I attended the same university at about the same time. The problem was we were in two different colleges at our university and I almost never even ran into her among the thirteen thousand students that would race across the hilly terrain of Florida A&M.

Finally, I met her, a medium-built black girl who organized for Obama. We introduced ourselves to each other and our connection was made immediately. She was originally from Waterloo, Iowa, and left the Corn State to venture into Florida to attend the nation's largest historically black college or university at Florida A&M. Because of our connection to the university, she and I vowed that we would never disrespect each other or treat each other maliciously, no matter what the outcome for our candidates. We wouldn't play tricks to sway people and we would play politics above the belt. Over time, she would give me insight into events that I needed to be at. But that was the extent of her help and I was and still am eternally grateful for her unwavering support of me.

You see, organizing has a way of taking you on a roller-coaster ride. There are a lot of twists and turns, ups and downs. You can enjoy the ride or fear it, but the journey you're on is sure to be the ride of your life.

CHAPTER 4

THE ROLE THAT MY RACE PLAYED

Hillary Clinton didn't mind talking about her run as it pertained to women's history. Barack Obama hesitated to use the historicalness of his run as the premise for his wanting to advance to the White House. They both made choices about how they might include or disclude race and gender on the campaign trail. Personally, I felt I deserved to make the same decision for myself as well but I never had that prerogative because when I, a black woman, discussed supporting Hillary Clinton, a white woman, over Barack Obama, a black man, all that mattered was race or gender, and I had the responsibility of telling why I had chosen to support one over the other. The explanation was never the problem; it was the reaction to it that made things tough. Oftentimes, when I'd finished explaining my point of view to black people, they were disgusted; when I would talk to white people, especially men, they were outraged, and it just ended up making me confused. I wasn't working to please people about my decision; I was working and organizing to help people support my candidate. So I always wondered why my race or gender, for that matter, played any significant role in organizing. And, honestly, the feeling of isolation after explaining why I had decided to support one over the other didn't happen to me SOME of the time; this happened to me ALL of the time.

I saw glimpses of this while I was in college as I would gather my friends for my usual potluck and politics meeting of the minds at my house or at a local eatery. We would have fabulous discussions on who was the ideal candidate and it almost always came down to Clinton or Obama. In fact, during these awesome exchanges of political feasting, I had never really made up my mind about whom I was going to support. It was too much of a sticky situation to decide between Hillary Clinton, a brilliant, astute stateswoman, or an equally brilliant, astute statesman; the situation was that the differences were so microscopic that if you put both of their senatorial experiences on a résumé and covered their names, there would be no significant difference. I mean my chest was filled with pride over Barack Obama being able to address the DNC members at a general session when John Kerry was running for president. This man didn't just step up on the stage; he owned it. I felt like his speech connected me to what I should be concerned about and it was not partisan politics or looking at our country as this blue or red state; he focused my attention on working together as the United States of America. So I held, and still do hold, Mr. Obama in very high esteem. But to some, I was just plain on slave working for "massa" Hillary by selecting to support Clinton over Obama. Don't get me wrong: a little fun bantering back and forth never hurt a soul, but to hear someone describe my commitment to supporting Hillary Clinton on the same level as a slave/master relationship was truly despicable. My friends have a way of showing passion by taking personal aim, and they made sure that the point was clear that I was still on the plantation and I now had the political freedom to select any person on my own, so why was I so dead-set on being loyal to the "Clinton brand"? I've never had to defend such a personal decision in my life, let alone one that wasn't a poor choice, but the onus was always on me to explain why I was selling Obama out. Why couldn't I join Mrs. Obama in being proud of our country? I was brainwashed by mainstream America. All of it was very far from the truth and I had to keeps people's baseless rhetoric in line with the reality of the situation.

Hillary Clinton had a true track record that I fully support; she had given me tangible evidence of what she could do once she had the position to maneuver the power. She had dealt with the pressures of Washington and emerged still standing. Mr. Obama was a newcomer; although I wasn't skeptical of his promises, I decided to place my bets on a competitor that I'd seen win and not on someone who dreamed of winning. Turned out my theory was WAY OFF but my rationale never came down to this heartbreaking battle over selecting someone who identified with my culture or someone who identified with my gender. I really didn't care that Hillary Clinton was a woman and I cared a lot that Mr. Obama was biracial; I just didn't believe that he would get the institutional support to carry him to the finish line. Hillary was raising money hand over fist and Obama was trying to get his operation rocking and rolling. Hillary Clinton's campaign came off as polished and prepared for battle and the Obama campaign seemed to rely on grass-roots organizing that you don't see much of beyond local elections, but it worked…and it worked well enough to put him in the White House.

What I ultimately felt were Hillary's strengths turned out to be major weaknesses for what one wanted to accomplish. While I viewed Obama's organizing game plan as innovative, it concerned me that he wasn't following the traditional rule book, but what I learned along the way was that he was literally changing the game, and this is from the perspective of having the sheer pleasure of working for both organizations. None of this made any difference when I was confronted with the question of why I was supporting Clinton over Obama, and I never explained it in those terms. Hell, I ran like Harriet Tubman away from the race question, but I couldn't run far when I had to go and canvass. Canvassing was always interesting for this organizer; aside from being afraid of dogs, the second thing I dreaded the most was answering the question of why I chose Hillary over Obama.

Let me put this in context for you; there were several people running during the primary: Biden, Edwards, Kunich, and the list goes on. But I didn't get the question of why Clinton over Biden (that's easy: electability), or Edwards over Clinton. I always got "why Clinton over the big O" and when I did, it made me cringe and think to myself, *OH, SHIT!*

One day as I was canvassing, I knocked on the door of a white woman in one of the precincts that I managed. She came to the door and talked about the war, and said that she supports women running for office because men were insensitive dogs. She hated seeing Edwards drag his sick wife to Iowa; she felt his attempt to win office was insincere, that Bill Richards wasn't equipped to lead the nation, and that

Joe Biden talked too much, so I was waiting for her to give her thoughts on Obama so that I could get her to sign a supporter card for Hillary, invite her to an event, and get her rocking and rolling on the campaign trail. She stopped at Obama and said that there was something different about him. *Oh, lord, here it comes: these people are drinking the punch.* Normally I didn't let people go on and on about Obama; when they started singing his praises, I asked them if they had to choose today, would they stand for hope, which was his biggest theme in Iowa, or demand leader-ship that would change things. I never used names, just metaphors, to make a point. She interrupted me and point-blank asked why a black girl wasn't in support of Obama. *Lady, you've got to be kidding me! If I told you I was sup-porting Obama because he was black, you would criticize my rationale, so why in the hell are you asking me this?* I just stood there fearful that I would let my true thoughts run out of my mouth. In response to her question, I requested that she give me one reason Hillary Clinton should stand in line for office behind anybody that has proven themselves like she has. "Everyone has their reason for supporting a candi-date. I am asking you to support mine based on what she can tangibly do to and for our country in the White House." She stopped me suddenly to remind me that Obama would be the first black president and that was something to be proud of. I laughed because frankly that accomplishment of being the first black president would only benefit him. His race wouldn't change that we were facing the worst of times, and while people saw it symbolically as a treasured asset, I considered it as a resource that he would not be able to use when fighting on our behalf.

It seems like I could never get the race or gender thing right. No matter what I said or how I put things, some people were either from that feat and their accomplishments on a résumé and cover their names using the naked eye or basic human intuition, you can't see the damn difference. And things didn't change.

Shocking ignorance I cannot explain my contempt for the imperfect. It takes courage to answer questions that you have no explanation for since there is a chance that the point you arrive at could be wrong; it's a sign of wisdom to take a look and be silent to absorb the information. On many days, I felt the pain of not having an answer and the pressure of not knowing what to say. My mission made my answer inferior to people's questions and ultimately I amassed a feeling of bitterness for not being able to vocalize a response that appeased people's perspectives about my support for one candidate over the other. In truth, there was no code for the rationale behind my selecting Hillary Clinton, outside of the reality that during the time I decided that I would journey away from friends and family to place a hardworking Democrat in the White House. It made sense to support the person who was raising money hand over fist and had the support of leaders whose world view I respected. I've never had to justify why I supported Edwards over Kerry or Gore over Bradley. I viewed the questioning of my choice to support Clinton instead of Obama as an illustration that no answer meant no support.

The gravity of this responsibility changed my view on the role race plays in electoral politics. What I learned was that I had to provide a response, and yet truly it never was the right answer.

CHAPTER 5

NOT ANOTHER REQUEST FOR A BACKYARD BARBECUE

I owa is full of people who love the political process. I mean, if you didn't like it, you had to love it because participating meant giving something that you can never get back: TIME. To take several hours out of your life to go and participate in a process calling caucusing was no small feat, but what it took to get a person to go and stand up in your corner and be counted meant spending countless hours and resources getting to know the voter. That in itself typified a program that I was not familiar with at all since, in Florida, we go to a poll where the process is not public; it's public participation in a private process. Though we celebrate our support of candidates, it's generally in a manner where hundreds or in some cases thousands can gather and rally, but not in Iowa. On most occasions, people who wanted to touch or feel the candidate would do something that I found odd or downright unusual: they would request that you bring the person you were organizing for to their local diner, their community gathering, their church event, or, in many cases, their house, where friends and family, neighbors and community leaders would gather around with a cup of coffee and a slice of humble pie to ask the tough questions in an environment that was anything other than casual since this cadre of the community had come together to take care of business.

I had no political understanding of the culture of the Iowa caucus and how connected the people became with the candidate; at first it fascinated me then it frightened me. The requests were generally simple but providing accommodations would mean hours upon hours of laborers and resources just to attend a ten-minute shindig, and in many cases people would inform me that if my candidate didn't come to their backyard barbecue, their support would lean in the opposite direction because, as I learned full well, Iowans don't take your word—they listen to the words of the candidate, interview them for the job, and then support them wholeheartedly, even at the expense of losing the precious commodity of time to support their choice. I would agonize over invitations as if I made the decision for Hillary Clinton to attend events, wondering what the higher-ups would say if I forwarded them an email that Sweet Susie wanted Hillary over for tea. It become clear to me that these requests were not overlooked and, in most cases, much was done to get Hillary to these local events. And if she couldn't make it, you could be having dinner with the likes of Sec. Albright, Stephanie Tubbs Jones, or Terry McCulliffe—not such a bad trade-off. The beauty of this system was that, no matter what, people got to see the candidates in a different way, away from the lights, the camera, or the actions. It was very unplugged, raw, and real.

There was a local activist in Waterloo who worked extremely hard fighting for justice; as a matter of fact, her work dated back to the civil rights era. Mrs. Anna Mae Weems was a powerhouse and from the minute I met her, she seem to exude a concern for the community that she tended to vocalize each time she would cross paths with anyone who met her. This woman, in short, was a dynamic drum leader for change. During the '50s, she worked hard to bring Dr. Martin Luther King to Waterloo, and when he left she carried on his mantel of fighting for justice and equality for residents of the Cedar Valley area with an enormous amount of pride and resiliency. Even in 2007, she was still a vocal fighter. Mrs. Weems, who at the time of our meeting was in her budding eighties, was still plugged in politically. I wasted no time in trying to connect with her. The funny thing is she invited me over several times, and each time she would school me all about Waterloo but I would leave with no commitment of her support. It was always impor- tant to me that I shared my story as to why I was supporting Hillary Clinton and I desperately wanted her to see my point of view so that she would at least consider supporting my choice as well. When it came down to it, she was down- right torn as to whom she wanted to support. At times, she admired the charisma of Barack Obama and yet enjoyed the incredible strength of Hillary Clinton. I don't believe I had anything to do with shaping her opinion one way or the other for Hillary Clinton because, as she would put it, she could make up her own mind.

However, she was one of the folks who were straightfor- ward and adamant about meeting Hillary Clinton. Her oppor- tunity arrived when Clinton came to Waterloo to address the local union in the area. After the event, there was a small round-table discussion for a select group of local activists and Mrs. Weems was one of those who attended this event. I sat silently in the back of the room, eyeing Mrs. Weems all along to see her reaction to the questions being asked. The meeting seemed to work its magic; the interviewed was conducted and Hillary Clinton, as she always does, sealed the deal. Crossing my fingers, I hoped that figuratively, Mrs. Weems had hired her. After Mrs. Clinton left the room, it was clear that Mrs. Weems was on board. It felt good to clinch the support of such a highly visible activist.

Days after the event, I found myself attending those barbecues, sounding the alarm that Ana Mae Weems was now on Hillary Clinton's team. Maybe her support would convince folks that it was okay to break rank and really decide who they were going to support. My approach worked the exact opposite charm. People were clearly disillusioned with my news and eventually folks began to muster up the courage to say things that troubled me. It was brought to my attention that Mrs. Weems wasn't a real Hillary Clinton supporter at all. At that point, I refused to believe the hearsay because there was no clear evidence that she was anything other than a Clinton supporter. So I took the words of a single individual with a grain of salt and kept moving on. I chose to ignore those people but their voices didn't mute because I was no longer listening; they just grew a little stronger. In the end, it seemed that I was happiest that Mrs. Weems declared her support of Clinton.

One day an active supporter of the Hillary Clinton local campaign asked to speak with me. This individual was one of the sweetest people you could meet but on that day she put no sugar on what she wanted to announce to me.

As we sat, she reminded me that she was a Hillary Clinton supporter before it was popular for people in the African-American community to even consider supporting her and she supported Hillary even when people ostracized her for her outspoken support. She never wanted anything from the campaign; all she wanted was Hillary in the White House. I looked at her and knew that her unhappiness was frustrating. She went on to say that while she didn't care who was supporting Hillary, she felt that the campaign overlooked her support and didn't do enough to appreciate all that she was doing. I took a deep breath because it was hard hearing her express this sort of discomfort. Then she laid the biggest bombshell ever on me that Anna Mae Weems was a signed supporter of Barack Obama. So now I was hearing from a different voice the same news! Then she said, "Everyone in the community knows it except you." That took the complete wind out of me.

I tried to convince her that this wasn't true. I even admitted that Mrs. Weems had mentioned time and time again during our conversation that she had supported Obama at one time and it was okay for a person to change their mind. I was desperate to find out the root of this commotion. I didn't want to go to another gathering where people backed me into a corner to share their thoughts about Anna Mae Weems' support. Then she handed me a folded piece of paper. I quickly opened it and, at the top, read the phrase: "Obama Campaign Announces African-American Steering Committee." I held my breath as I looked down the paper and, sure enough, Anna Mae Weems' name was listed on Obama literature as a member of the African-American Steering Committee. I sat there and tried to figure out what to do—not what to do about the situation, but what to do next. She helped me out when she just exited the room with a quiet, "We'll talk later."

I was dumbfounded. I shot an email off to several people in the campaign to make them aware of the chatter. Then I needed to clear my head so I left the office and found myself meeting with my dear friend Maria, the Obama organizer. We talked and exchanged pleasantries. Then I eased into why I wanted to speak with her. I'd call the meeting to see if she could give me any clear indications of the relationship her organization had with Mrs. Weems. For me, finding out was a priority not because I wanted to wage a battle or create a big fuss but I just wanted to get a clearer picture of what I was dealing with and I wanted to end the barbecue gossiping about the whole ordeal. Maria was perhaps caught off guard when I made the intentions for my meeting clear. She said something that spoke volumes to me and positioned me to leave that room sure about what I was dealing with. The way she put it was frank: people had choices. Not everyone we started with ended with us and not everyone that starts on one side will end up staying in your corner. People have choices. No matter what decision Mrs. Weems made, conventional or not, it was now my responsibility to use her support to help Hillary Clinton.

Frustrations began to simmer and barbecues went back to being an environment where people could grill me about the candidate instead of blowing out the flames of frustrations over key supporters.

CHAPTER 6

THE HARKIN STEAK FRY

The Harkin steak fry is one of the most important events to attend and participate in, especially if you are trying to solicit support from Iowans who go and caucus. The event is sponsored by one of Iowa's treasured and tenured politicos: Senator Tom Harkin.

During my work on the 2007 caucus, I was enthusiastic about going out to this sort of field of dreams for presidential contenders. You see, candidates had a chance to work the crowd and talk to people face to face, which was altogether common when it came to Iowa. The magic, though, wasn't in touching people at this large event; it was in taking that good ole backyard barbecue feel and multiplying it to the tenth power so that several thousand people could enjoy great food and a display of democracy in action: a sort of potluck and politics feel.

I never imagined that rolling out to Indianola would give me the second wind I needed to soar to the end of this race, but it did. So when our statewide campaign operation beckoned its organizers and paid staff from all across the state to our central headquarters, I was excited to hit the road once again. Hillary Clinton organizers poured into Des Moines, Iowa, from all over to be led by our fearless leader, none other than Ms. Teresa Vilmain. Teresa is not what you would expect to see after hearing her story. She's not a cold-hearted, stony, ice-cold bitch. Her character screams "woo-sah" as she floats around a room to pick your brains on how you're implementing the campaign's strategy and if you are one of those who inadvertently express some message that doesn't coincide with what she wants, her disappointment turns into a teachable moment since she's always on the lookout to help folks move beyond their mistakes to learn. So no screaming and yelling, no loud talking. She's direct, she's assertive, but she looks like a quirky yoga instructor. In short, she was different. But her difference made it easier to like her.

This was not my first time interacting with her but it was my first time seeing her flawlessly put her plan into action and work the room, even if it was a room full of her campaign's organizers. For this particular assignment, she made the mission clear as she reviewed the goals we needed to hit at the Harkin steak fry. We were there to get supporters! The assignment seemed easy enough but the strategy was a little different. She wanted us to be the polite campaign, the campaign that didn't argue, and, most importantly, wasn't rude.

The atmosphere in Iowa from the moment I arrived was that the local people felt as though the campaigns and the campaigning had started all too fast. Most people argued that since the caucus was more than several months away, there was no reason to call as excessively as we did and no reason to pin them down to a candidate right away. I believe that Teresa took the sentiments and made a valiant effort to address those concerns by changing the approach of our campaign for that particular event. We would share our story of why we joined the campaign, we would talk about supporting our candidate, we would test the individual to see if they had selected a candidate, and go in for the hard ask. Typically, if a caucus-goer mentioned that they were possibly for another candidate, I would try to break down their support of that candidate by discussing issues that were important to them and discussing where Hillary stood on those issues, or talk about her record in Congress as a senator. But none of that was appropriate for the steak fry because, like Teresa said, we were the nice campaign.

While in the headquarters, we went over what areas we would be assigned to and what role we would play. Then Teresa recruited an organizer who admitted that she was a former cheerleader to teach us a few campaign chants. Within a few minutes, we had a chant that stuck: "I-O-W-A, Hilary Clinton all the way!" I scrambled to get the feel of the rhythmic words so that I could really chant my support of Hillary with conviction. Things were going along fine then Teresa pulled a doozy: she said that we would create music by pounding on buckets purchased from Home Depot. What? She couldn't be serious! I mean I love music, but playing drum beats on the barrel of a bucket totally changed the purpose of showing enthusiasm to looking erratic. Imagine walking up to a family picnic and having some person pretend that they are playing drums by beating on a pot and then wanting to talk to you about something as serious as caucusing? I can't speak for all, but to me it was a joke. It didn't matter what I thought, though, because I was there to do it and so I did.

That morning, we would all rise early and go from Des Moines to Indianola to put up Hillary Clinton yard signs. It was dark as we were driving into town but as the dawn of day came over the horizon, as far as my eyes could see there were huge, gigantic, oversized Obama campaign signs that read "HOPE." I was aghast at the sheer sight of these signs; they were everywhere, on every corner, and there were very few if any Hillary Clinton ones. As I recall the memories of that sight, I remember where I got my energy from to start placing our yard signs everywhere. All you could see were organizers running from car trunks carrying yard signs and putting them in the ground. Now the battle was on because as we got closer to the field where the steak fry would take place, it was an all-out battle or sign war. We placed Hillary Clinton placards everywhere. To get to the top of high walls, we placed people on the necks or backs of each other and we had our human nail guns tacking those placards up—and that was all before nine in the morning.

We all regrouped and started to get ready to hand out free water, popcorn, and other goodies, or what the campaign referred to as "chum," so that people could get nice novelty items with our candidate's name on it. The night before I may have been slightly tuned off by the buckets we were using as drums, but I picked up a drum and started beating the hell out of it as I yelled, "I-O-W-A, Hillary Clinton all the way" with energy and power that was left over from earlier that morning after seeing all of that Obama signage. Teresa's idea was unconventional but it worked; we were getting so many supporter cards that we had to literally take them back to our makeshift on-site headquarters using our bucket drums. And people did see us as the nice campaign team. I would laugh as people would walk up to the narrow walkway that led them inside the event and another campaign with their organizers would rush the person down and the person would freak out.

There were times when a Hillary Clinton supporter would be engaging a potential caucus-goer about our candidate and organizers from the opposing side would try to run up and talk at the same time; again, people would freak out and then be turned off, but not by us. The cherry on top of the cake was that outside of a few Edwards organizers, no other campaign had shown up in full force and really it looked like we were running the show. That moment, however, didn't last long because, from nowhere, the Obama campaign responded. From a distance I could see hundreds of people walking with Barack Obama from the road as we stood at the entrance of the gate. As they got closer, I could see that it was not only Barack Obama but also his wife and a band comprised of real drummers.

People inside the event begin to hear the drummers as well and made a bee line to the gates to get a closer look. This time, instead of the caucus-goers freaking out, I was beginning to unravel. There I stood, looking like an overzealous loony-toon with a big "H" painted on the side of my face that was now beginning to run down my cheek from the sweat that the heat caused, and I still had my silly makeshift drum in hand. I wanted to start chanting but how could one compete with the style of their entrance? It was sheer genius. I swear, as I stood there, I felt like I was now a part of the Barack Obama campaign show.

As soon as they crossed the walkway, they started chanting those infamous words: "FIRED up! Ready to go!" My mouth dropped. They stole our damn thunder but their shenanigans for that day weren't over. They kept marching, screaming and shouting, and chanting; at one point I was sure that Obama was going to make a detour and leave to some holding spot, but he marched right in with his supporters and seemed to be enjoying it. He marched with his supporters inside the event, away from any holding room, and then he did what all Iowans really want: he started working that field like he was networking a room, talking one-on-one with caucus-goers.

It was time to shift gears so we ran inside the gates because the steak fry was about to begin and we still had work to do. The first thing was to watch Senator Harking and Hillary Clinton toss steak on the grill while every news camera imaginable took live footage of the feat. As her supporters, we hooped and hollered for her and then it was off again to get near the stage so that when she spoke, we could do the same. I raced back so that I could get as close to the stage as possible. The crowd was enormous now and it was hard to find a spot but I did.

The first business of order at the event was to have some of the candidates come to the stage and participate in the Pledge of Allegiance. As we stood there, it occurred to me that Barack Obama didn't have his hand planted across his chest. I was astonished, but honestly I thought that maybe the reason he didn't was because the flag was behind him and he wasn't facing it. Whatever his reason was, several people standing near me were completely perturbed by his gesture. One lady asked me for a supporter card and said his actions helped her make her final choice. I handed her the pin and the card with mixed emotions.

Then the show began. First it was Dodd, then Richardson, then Biden, on to Edwards, and finally my girl, Hillary Clinton. The applause as she approached the stage was thunderous. She spoke eloquently and did an amazing job in her message at invoking the spirit of why she decided to run for president. I screamed and yelled from the audience and before she left the stage, supporters and organizers alike all chanted, "*I-O-W-A, Hillary Clinton all the way!*" She exited the stage and a small thought ran through my mind: *How would Iowans respond to Obama now, since he had not displayed his patriotism?* The answer to that question was unlike what I would have ever imagined. As he took the stage and positioned himself at the podium, hundreds upon hundreds of people began to whip out the famous O-shaped Obama placards with the American flag in the middle of the "O." When I glanced around, it was clear that an overwhelming majority of the people standing on the grounds of the Harkin steak fry were waving this Obama placard—and to make things worse, he got them to repeat the chant, "Fired up and ready to go," and when they did, you would have thought that the Harkin steak fry turned into an Obama rally. I yelled our chant but the voices of our supporters were drowned out by the massive Obama organization.

The event ended and as we pulled down signs along the highway, it was evident that we may have been the nice campaign but Obama was the organized group. His team had done a good job of showing the nation that he was organized in Iowa and the strength of his organization showed that he could contend and win. Even after see-ing his strength, it was still hard for me to recognize that a weakness even existed in the Hillary Clinton organization. I made excuses: we had older people, they did not; we had reliable caucus-goers, he had groupies; we had heart, they had hype. So I rolled out of the steak fry with conviction in my heart that Clinton was still on top and that she would win the caucus.

The mood of the campaign team was more or less the same as mine. Sure, the Harkin steak fry was a battle, but we were all in it to win it and no one gives up at the first sign of danger.

It was quiet in the car riding back to the headquarters. Half of it had to do with the fact that we were all tired; the other half, I believe, was that we were still in awe of what we saw. A fellow co-worker broke the silence with an awkward statement that was haunting: "If he thinks he can depend on young people to caucus in order to win, then he's crazy because I didn't caucus in college and I am from here." I swear the sentiments of those very words came back and haunted us because both young and old came out and made history.

CHAPTER 7

HERE COME THE SURROGATES

The caucus was drawing near and friends and even family members of Hillary Clinton began to pour into the state of Iowa as the organization ratcheted up its force of organizing on the ground. The support was following and the supporters were hyped, which meant that they were sending Hillary Clinton to every possible corner of Iowa. Since she's just one person, but the message of why you should support her needed to be heard, this meant that the surrogates would now be sent out to fish for any support.

Honestly, in my neck of the woods in Waterloo, Iowa, the number of surrogates that came through our area never slowed down and it only got crazier when November and December rolled around. I really liked seeing the surrogates interact with the voters; they all had their own individual strengths that made seeing them in action intriguing. One of these people was the late Stephanie Tubbs Jones. She was a fierce and loyal supporter of Hillary Clinton when the cameras were on and the newspaper writers were out, and was just as loyal when no one was watching.

They sent her to Waterloo, Iowa, and she was downright amazing. The first thing she wanted to do was get to the people. She jumped in my car and gave me the marching orders. We went to local eateries and she sipped coffee with local people and shared her experiences with Hillary Clinton. Although she was a celebrated congresswoman, she never came off with any airs; she simply introduced herself by stating her full name and leaving off the "congresswoman" part. She did that not because she had anything to hide; it was just her way of relating to people.

We went to the barbershop in the black community and that's when I really saw her brilliance at work. As we drove up, there was Obama signage on the window. She looked at the sign and then at me and I knew what that look indicated: she wanted me to bring in some Hillary Clinton placards and so I grabbed them and dashed up to the door. I was finally around someone who had the nerve to deal with supporters in an environment where it wasn't controlled. We were basically racing into the lion's den and although I had been in there dozens of times, it never stopped me from re-entering; in fact, it felt good to have some back-up with me, and there was no turning back. As soon as I hit the door, I saw the faces of the guys that knew me light up because they loved to pick my brain about Hillary Clinton and I never let them down. But as Rep. Tubb Jones stepped in behind me, they looked puzzled. She had to see their reaction and I knew she felt the sting of their glare, but she didn't miss one beat. She came in and introduced herself as a Hillary Clinton supporter and then handed each of them a plac-ard. I chuckled (even now) looking at their faces because they couldn't believe her nerve.

She looked at the Obama sign and then asked the owner if there was room for Hillary on the wall. He said yes and after I posted a sign, she asked them the question that set off the entire barbershop: "Is there room for you to support Hillary on caucus night?" All hell broke loose; most of them said no and even asked why she was supporting Hillary Clinton over Barack Obama. That didn't distract her from her mission of coming out of the barber shop with at least a supporter card from the anti-Clinton crowd. She didn't budge; she told them that she worked with both Clinton and Obama, and one of them asked for her support and the other tried to depend on it. Then she told the man, "And now I am asking for your support for Hillary Clinton. she'll ask for your vote and not just depend on you to support her.."

By this time, somebody had to have alerted the local Obama organizer that we were there because Maria, the Waterloo Obama organizer, came sliding through the door. Rep. Tubb Jones was unrelenting and people ate her up. Before we left that shop, we had passed out placards for Hillary Clinton, collected a couple of supporter cards, and she was giving out her email address and cell phone number so that some guy could get the recipe to her famous baked macaroni and cheese and her turkey dressing. I was on cloud nine because she showed up.

That evening, we headed to the NAACP dinner in Waterloo and people were drawn to her magnetism. We knew that we were dealing with a pretty committed crowd of Obama supporters but she worked that room like everyone there was in support of Hillary Clinton. Honestly, she energized me. But she wasn't alone; there were others like Rep. Shelia Jackson Lee. Although she was a member of Congress and a colleague of both Hillary Clinton and Stephanie Tubbs Jones, her approach was different but her level of support was just as personal and strong. During the summer, she came to Waterloo to participate in a parade that was held on the Eastside hosted by the KBBG family, the black management group that operated the public radio station. Our station or spot in the parade was sort of in the middle but she got out of the truck we had and did more than wave her hand to the folks that she barely knew; she also waved supporter cards and worked to get people to join her in supporting Hillary Clinton.

Her style was different when she was behind the scenes on down time; she was absorbed in reading or jotting down ideas. She didn't take any stuff when it came to handling her and advancing her steps; she had a particular way that she liked to do things but when she was on, she was on, and she shined brightly.

I worked two other events with her: one where I saw her walk into a room with minsters and, truth be told, there weren't many there, especially since so many had at this point committed to Barack Obama. It didn't matter because she spoke to them as if she were addressing four hundred people instead of maybe just four. She was one of the surrogates who didn't just share her story of how she worked with Hillary; she, unlike many others, would leave with a charge to support Hillary. After she was done, she would pull you to the side and start a conversation on what she saw and what she felt needed to be worked on, but it never interfered with her doing what she was asked to do.

One surrogate that was sent out was an attorney, Reta Lewis, and she was phenomenal, especially when she walked into my office, asked for a walk sheet, and walked the neighborhood. Anthony Brown was another person like that. He came with his own entourage and his chief of staff, and at first that seemed like a clear sign that he just wanted a microphone and podium placed in front of him, an instant crowd, and cheering. But he wasn't the type that wanted the show to be about him and making him feel good. He came because he was meeting a need and the need was to get out more caucus-goers in favor of Hillary. He was a black man who favored Obama and was in support of Hillary, so I made sure that we visited the barber shops because men have a way of connecting with each other and I was sure that he could give the fellas in the barber shop his own personal perspective as to why he was supporting Hillary that would ease anyone's fears about doing the same.

He also willingly knocked on doors and made phone calls. He didn't leave the office until the volunteers did and, above all, he was gracious; he never made people around him feel rushed as they shared their concerns with him. I saw this in a more intimate way as one of the people whom he spoke with, a local reverend, expressed his disgust and concerns with Lt. Gov. Brown. Rev. Loggins was between supporting Hillary Clinton and Barack Obama. His wife was surely on our side but he was not so sure what he wanted to do. I always knew that while Rev. Loggins was not a signed supporter of the campaign, he was not committed to any other campaign. It was suggested that maybe Lt. Gov. Brown could do a one-on-one with him and convince him to come on board.

As we drove up to the site where we would have our coffee klatsch, I didn't realize that the conversation would expose Rev. Loggins' feelings concerning how he viewed the campaign. We all sat down. Rev. Loggins listened to Gov. Lt. Brown and his pitch, and then moved that all aside to vent. He was unhappy because he felt that the campaign had done little to nothing to reach out to the black community and that we had taken his wife's support of Hillary Clinton for granted. He expressed that it was difficult supporting Hillary Clinton in a community where everyone else was pretty much on board with Obama, yet she did it anyway and she never got invited to meet Hillary herself. If this were any other state, his comments would have come across as childish, but we were in Iowa, where the caucus served as the appropriate measure for requesting unusual things like having coffee with the candidate.

He also believed that not enough information was sent into the community that was germane to the African-American community. He disclosed that the Obama campaign had a heavy presence in the African-American community because the office was on the Eastside; while our office was just up the street, it was in downtown Waterloo and therefore not as accessible. Lt. Brown listened to his concerns and, for a minute, I thought to myself, *I am going to have to jump in and start BS-ing so I won't have to put the lieutenant governor in a position to provide a response just to give the reverend an answer.* Before I could execute my move, Lt. Gov. Brown was already talking to Rev. Loggins, acknowledging his concerns and communicating our strengths. He didn't delegitimize the man and he didn't bullshit him, either; he connected with him on a common ground and moved the conversation forward.

The only other person I've witnessed doing the exact same thing with an enormous amount of ease was former president Bill Clinton. On the last hard push of the campaign, he came to town again—and he came with Magic Johnson. Our national African-American Outreach Team was making inroads into the African-American community of Waterloo. They sent out additional staff, which meant more boots on the ground and more support. But they were also responsible for coordinating events like having President Clinton come to town. President Clinton had an amazing way of working an audience; those piercing blue eyes, his presidential swagger, and Southern charm could instantly shift the atmosphere in a room where people were mostly guarded. When he came to speak at the Boys' and Girls' Club in Waterloo, it was my job to have supporter cards and pens ready so that after he shook a person's hand, I was lock-step behind him to ask for their support.

Even though it was maybe his first or second time meeting some of these people, I had interacted with them for months, knew their demeanor, and understood their disposition. So I was enthusiastic that so many people were breaking our way after he would shake their hand; they were game for inching closer to supporting Hillary Clinton.

CHAPTER 8

NATIONAL OFFICE SENDING IN THE CALVARY

The minute things started to look up and it seemed that we would be making strides in the community to connect candidate Clinton with caucus-goers, something would inevitably go haywire.

For weeks and months, folks would never truthfully admit that they had decided to support a candidate other than Hillary. Sometimes they would leave me warning signs that they weren't ready to commit. I would call and get no answer, as if I had just started cold-calling all over again—sign. I would meet with them and they would say things like, "If I participate in the caucus…" or "Maybe everyone else has decided but I still need to sort things out"—another sign! Or the big doozy: I would have a signed supporter card from an individual, they would come to all of our Hillary Clinton events, and I would attend a community event on behalf of the campaign, and the person in question would have on a Obama button. When I would inquire about the button, they would say things like, "They gave it to everyone at the door" or "My wife wears Hillary stuff when we go to your events and she isn't supporting her"—CLEAR sign. Well, nothing was clearer than leaving my office to travel to the Eastside of Waterloo, Iowa, and walking into my very own local version of a sign war.

For months on end, I would see no Obama signage anywhere. I would place Hillary Clinton yard signs in the ground anywhere I could and, once in a while, I would have a person or two allow me to place a sign in their yard. Ironically, these signs were repeatedly taken from people's yards. But I nonetheless would never see Obama signage. At one point, it was rumored around the community that if you wanted an Obama yard sign, you had to make a contribution. Most people baulked at the idea of buying a yard sign when every other campaign would freely give them to the person that was willing to accept them. Clearly people were peeved at the idea of paying—at least that's what they conveyed to me.

In Iowa, to have caucus-goers pay for campaign merchandise, otherwise known as chum, like what they give sharks as bait, must have been an immoral sin because people were aghast at the thought of this request, especially since they never had to shell out one cent for big-ticket statewide political events. I think over time the Obama team developed a message that made their decision to collect donations for buttons and yard signs work because people saw their donation help to reach out to others, and any time you breathe or speak the outreach, just know it takes reaching into pockets. However, none of this mattered.

I was driving while on the phone, listening in on a conference call, and I hit the first light that brought me into Eastside Waterloo. For as far as my eye could see, there were Obama yard signs everywhere; this was a sign that I could not ignore. It meant so many different things on so many different levels, but what was clear was that if the yard signs were any indication as to whom people were caucusing for, then my team was up shit's creek because I could hardly see any Hillary Clinton campaign yard signs peeking through the sea of signs that had "HOPE" plastered on them.

Instead of giving in to freaking out, I road in and out and all around East Waterloo, and, in total, I counted more than two hundred and thirty-seven yard signs to Hillary's thirty-nine—yes, just thirty-nine. Yet I didn't cry in despair or run to the office in a fit of rage and grab every yard sign available and place them on busy intersections and/or corners. I took notes and made observations and then the next thing I did was send emails to alert the team of the disaster that seemed to await us, especially when I considered the win number I was given.

You see, the win number is the target number of caucus-goers each organizer had to get to go and caucus for one's candidate. In short, it identified how many caucus-goers were needed to win a particular percent. Apparently, these numbers were created by using information on previous years' caucus turnouts. In some areas, the number was as low as seven and in other areas, the number could be as great as thirty-two, but I never had a goal number of anything that was over one hundred for a single precinct.

The numbers game made absolutely no sense. It was flawed from its inception since it used overlays from previous caucus turnouts to generate what we needed to hit in order to win. However, this goal number did not take into consideration a number of things. For example, Obama was generating support among people who were caucusing for the first time and had never been involved in the process. More importantly, in the African-American community, though civic engagement is important, people's participation in the caucus process seemed to vary from caucus year to caucus year. In effect, the numbers seemed to ignore the fact that Waterloo had the highest concentration of African-Americans outside of Des Moines, and the reality of the situation was that this community would be more partial to participating in this process out of pride and admiration for Obama. In short, that data that was used didn't capture this important fact, which is why the numbers were low; someone didn't factor in that more people would be caucusing.

My experience working with the statewide organization exposed their insensitivity to the idiosyncrasies that would compel one to make the necessary changes to represent the fact that more people were registering to vote, and therefore the new registration numbers could have been used as solid indicators that unlikely voters may be going to caucus. These factors were somehow overlooked by virtue of the fact that the goal numbers were dismal. Plus the signs in the neighborhood said this to me: "We are caucusing and it's not for your gal."

Because of the community I was organizing in, I had been connected with the national office and placed in touch with the members of the African-American Outreach Team. Earlier on during the campaign, they were instrumental in setting up calls with prominent African-American supporters of Hillary and with activists who were weighing their choice and would benefit from hearing the stories of support from leaders who led people that looked like them, worked in communities similar to theirs, and who dealt with political, social, and economic disparities that were alike. This time, when they came calling, they knew without much detail the climate of the political landscape concerning African-America voters in Waterloo and the culture of how the statewide organization had treated losing the support of African-American supporters in this area. Eventually they sent down a team of folks with whom we could join together and turn things around. So the national office unleashed support like never before. The materials that now went to the homes of Africans-Americans had images that looked like them. I know that it may be hard to conceptualize why any of that matters, but when you consider that the alternative candidate had radio ads that directly addressed this demographic, that there was campaign information with him hugging a mother at the local church that minority caucus-goers attended, that they had buttons that would acknowledge their presence in the campaign ("African-Americans for Obama"), or that there was a statewide steering committee created by the campaign with every imaginable African-American political player in Iowa, it was hard to compete with all of that by countering with good information that had no connection to the issues the community was facing or images that they could identify with. It was a joke; we would go to a church and, of course, the Obama team was there. We would pass out general campaign literature and the difference in presentation was night and day: their material spoke directly to the people; ours spoke about the people.

Well, the national office had the ability to create the changes the community needed to see without sacrificing their support, as the statewide organization had done, and it came in the form of more boots on the ground, specialized strategists, and a core understanding of the diaspora of the community. Unfortunately, this didn't happen until about November, but in reality their help was significant. When I first met with the guys that came into town, I took them to the Eastside of Waterloo and told them that when I got there, people had not made up their minds about Obama and weren't sure about Hillary. Over time, people would commit to us here and there, but I never saw any evidence of support for Obama because house signs, my indicator of organizational support, were not present. Very few yards had any political signs, let alone an Obama one. Then Obama's organization rose like a phoenix out of the ashes and left us standing there in the dust with their yard signs everywhere. They took a look at what I was referencing and they realized that my concerns were valid.

People ate up the fact that Hillary Clinton had multiplied her African-American outreach, but it was too little too late. Frankly, they stopped the damage of an all-out massacre, but the victory was still won by the Obama team.

CHAPTER 9

THE IOWA JJ DINNER

I f the mood of the campaign was "we are in it to win it," by the time we got to the JJ, the atmosphere erupted with "let's win at all costs."

This was extremely evident in everything, down to messaging, organizing, and even the visibility of the campaign. No single cost was spared and, as always, when the political stakes were high, the Iowa Operation of the Hillary Clinton Presidential Exploratory Committee went all the way out, even if it was way in the wrong direction.

By this point of the game, I was numb to all of the "we will win" speeches because I was witnessing firsthand that the message was all hype in an effort to perhaps pysch our minds to believe that we were on track to win. Despite my own personal reservations over how the African-American community was archaically organized, there was no time to complain. In fact, the Iowa operation heads seemed to like organizers who would only open their mouths to praise their efforts, so I went back to my routine posture of keeping my face in the game and my mouth closed. Coming up for air meant heading down to Des Moines to support yet another statewide operation; in this instance, it was all hands on deck for the biggest political dinner of the year: the Iowa JJ.

Nationally recognized political commentators, operatives, consultants, and anyone worth their salt came down to add flavor to the festivities in hopes of getting their candidate positioned to meritoriously win the JJ. In others words, the campaign that had the best visibility, supporters, and speech by the candidate got the spoils of non-stop coverage of their triumph on local and national news, which is great since the event was the last, big-party, statewide event before the caucus. The thrill of being able to contribute to the last hurrah was exhilarating, so when the campaign operations team came calling, it was more than a treat to race down the icy Iowa highway from Waterloo to Des Moines.

As the team of Waterloo organizers left, we had no idea what we were in for, but as we approached the operations headquarters, it became clear that everyone, and I mean everyone, was there to work, no small talk or catching up with people that you only emailed a million times a day. It was all getting ready for the big dinner showdown.

As always, everyone gathered around in a huge circle as the ring leader of our circus came out to give us our charge before we got orders from other senior membership staff. On this occasion, Teresa was far more serious than I had ever seen her. From the moment she opened her mouth, all of could think was, *What?* Yep, the gravity of the situation clearly left my body as my decorum toward the discussion moved from anticipation to agitation. It seemed like, for the JJ, the campaign decided to test a new slogan and before I could ever get around to analyzing the phrase, I stood paralyzed at the hideous color of the new campaign chum. Don't get me wrong; I adore the color yellow, but match yellow with green and it just ends up looking like something a toddler shovels around on his plate of unwanted particles. It was puke-ish. This didn't seem to bother Teresa; her focus was gearing us up for a long night and day ahead. All the while I was trying to figure out why the campaign had made a U-turn in design effect and message for this event.

As if the colors didn't do enough to make you want to cut your eyes out, the phrase was equally unappealing; it read, "Turn up the HEAT and turn America around." I can still laugh in disbelief. Are you kidding me? Consider this:

Obama had largely dominated the phrase war with capti-
vating one-liners that went viral because people ascribed
their own meaning to them—for instance, his campaign's
usage of one-liners like "HOPE" and "CHANGE." I don't know
what they were thinking when the HRC machine came up
with "Turn up the HEAT and turn America around," but it
certainly fel flat.

I think the highlight of that night, other than getting my
directions and getting out of there, was having Chelsea
Clinton speak. She gave meaning to what this race meant
for the country, the state of Iowa, and, on a personal note,
herself. Chelsea Clinton is a powerhouse who spoke with
sincerity. After she walked out, the dark clouds gathered
again to rain down countless orders, one of which was the
sign war. We were to report to the venue early in the morning to check in and then move on to claim our space at the
sign war.

Unlike the Harkin steak fry, this time we were highly
armed with tons of signs and we had a real game plan. I
don't know when I actually left the building to go to sleep,
but when I did, it seemed like in a matter of moments it was
time to return to the trenches to fight again. It was bitterly
cold that morning, especially for a Southern girl like me, who
needs sunshine, clear skies, and eighty-degree tempera-
tures. As soon as check-in was over, we, every single Iowa
staff member of the campaign team, positioned ourselves

in strategic locations outside of the JJ dinner venue with our signs. Although we were not allowed to put up any posters yet, we had to stand in place so that the Obama campaign staff wouldn't be able to get a single piece of their signage anywhere near the entrance of the event.

In true campaign style, we young, bold, fearless, freezer-burnt political operatives begin to chant, "I-O-W-A, Hillary Clinton ALL THE WAY!" Then we shouted back and forth, "Turn up the heat, TURN America around!" As we did, media personnel began to come out and tape us, but, as good organizers, we never answered any formal questions. We were all just too happy to be there and truly to be there alone. There was no sign whatsoever of the Obama campaign, and I was thanking dear baby Jesus for that. In effect, we had the entire block on lock with our signs; even the car garage had Hillary Clinton signage all over it. Finally, we had won the sign war!

To thank us for standing there freezing our asses off in the cold, Teresa came around with the chairman of our national campaign, Terry McAuliffe, to thank us and pour us cups of coffee or hot chocolate. Meeting him there was crazy; it was like talking to a used car salesman—awkward. He had this huge smile on his face that went from one side to other and he, in addition to passing out coffee, was also passing out his book and signing it, no less. Lord, I thought, *What in the world is this man doing?* When he came to me,

I was waiting on the song and dance, the parade of super-ficiality, but what he gave instead was anything but that. I took his book and he signed it for me. Since I had nothing to lose, I raised the stakes and called my dad and asked him to say hi to my parents, who were all the way in Florida. He grabbed the phone and told them that I was working for the next president of the United States of America, Hillary Clinton. I laughed because my parents had decided that Obama was their man, so I knew that somehow my dad would probably mention that, and he did. Then Chairman McAuliffe went into full campaign mode, encouraging my dad to consider her record. The moment was summed up with his handing the phone back to me and jokingly saying, "Well, at least your family was smart enough to send you."

Things only began to get more entertaining after he left, books and all. That entire morning, the Clinton cam-paign was out in front of the venue all alone. But the closer it got to the time to be able to officially put up our signs, the more buzzed the entry became with signs of the Obama squad showing up, decked out in war paint on their faces, prepared to fight for space, but they lost the fight before they could even take position because, of course, we were ready for battle! The expressions on their faces screamed, "OH, SHIT!" We had every imaginable space on lock and the only thing that they could do was wait to see if we would move because, as the saying goes, "move your feet, lose your seat." So the staring match was going down. I laughed so hard watching the Obama operations team truck pull up with their big "HOPE" signs, scrambling to find alternative usage for all of their stuff.

In true Amanda form, I started taunting the organizers I knew from the Obama team, demanding they let me know if breakfast was good since they ran so late. Eventually they figured out what they were going to do. I knew this because some of their organizers started to squeeze between the Hillary Clinton organizers that were placed around a huge, oversized planter. At first we all made a big fuss, protesting that they showed up late and that it looked bad for the "Change Agents" to be stealing our space. But in actuality what they did was get a string of huge signs and create an elevated arch. Damn, why didn't we think about having somebody sit on a cloud to put our Hillary Clinton signs in the sky? Then when the whistle blew to let us start putting up our signs, we went crazy and, in about fifteen minutes flat, the Hillary Clinton team took the victory of the sign war. It was over.

The sore losers that they were, the Obama team got the yard signs and started putting them down on the ground. The move was pretty stupid because no one walking into the arena would see the signs against the backdrop of the

Hillary monstrosities everywhere, but we let them put their signs down. When they were done and cheering over their small victory, we put our signs right in front of or next to theirs. Then the sign war went to the street; at every car that went by, we chanted the pure heck out of them, screaming Hillary's name and all. To every other campaign, it was apparent that we stepped our game up since the steak fry.

Time went by so fast that day that as soon as we are done chanting and waving signs, it was time to gather inside the auditorium. The energy of the event gave me the strength to keep pushing on, even though I was tried. One thing missing was the Obama people. Now, I knew that they had given away tickets to the event because people were clambering to get one since superstar sensation Usher was doing a mini concert before the event. Turns out they were just running late because the Obama supporters came marching through the doors that led to the seating for the event, like ants all decked out in candy red shirts plastered with the catch phrase the Obama campaign was now using: "Fired UP, Ready to GO!" It didn't bother me at all because the size of their supporter section was similar to ours, plus we wore shirts as well. They were yellow and green shirts that read, "TURN UP the HEAT, TURN AMERICA AROUND!" We had a message; they used a slogan.

Hillary Clinton's fire that night was ferocious. As I sat in my seat, her words reminded me of why I had signed up to be in this battle, and though things looked challenging, I vowed to take the fight back to Waterloo without games or gimmicks. This event signaled the last major event before the caucuses, so it was time to fight and her words gave me the fire to keep things burning until the end.

CHAPTER 10

DEFEAT AT WATERLOO: HOW HILLARY LOST THE IOWA CAUCUS

The events of the political season were drawing to an end and now everything we had sincerely fought hard for was at stake.

The presence of the Iowa caucus seemed to exhaust me but on the day of the event, I was eerily underwhelmed by the casual way we went about conducting business. There were no speeches, no sign wars, no free events; it was just democracy in its purest form: people taking issues and making a decision to activate the process we know as civic engagement.

It's no surprise what happened that night. It grieved me severely that Hillary Clinton, my candidate and number-one choice for president, suffered a severe blow in losing the first presidential contest. A leader and trailblazer, she created an opportunity for women to be viewed as legitimate contenders for the office of president. If I had questions on what went wrong with the campaign and how she barely pulled third place in this political contest, I'm sure that she sure did, too. It was too hurtful to imagine, good or bad, that we could not pull a win for her. I believed for so long that perhaps the issue was disorganization, a top-heavy group of campaign managers, and America's predisposed notions of isolating the role of women in this country to certain roles of authority. If you'd ask me the question of why or how Hillary Clinton lost right after I completed my work on the campaign, I would have given you an explanation filled with all of the stories that I shared with you in this book as indicators that the outcome of the caucus shouldn't have been surprising at all.

In fact, these stories just legitimize my position that the consultants were out-of-touch, overpriced number-crunchers that didn't know how to connect their numbers to campaign and election strategy well enough to make the operation work and certainly win. My aggravation over the

results may have led me to disclose that the Iowa operation was mildly dysfunctional, with shifting leaders, feuding
department heads, and a consortium of half-baked, hare-
brained ideas that did nothing to support our goal of getting Hillary Clinton across the finish line and in the winning
column. The fact is I was too close to the pain of what I
had given my life to for several months, and even though
I could give an answer, no amount of explanation at the
time would adequately answer the question of how Hillary
Clinton lost the Iowa caucus.

In this sense, time is a true resource that brings a degree
of clarity. Though she lost, the reasons why have less to do
with the structure of her organization and more to do with
the ever-changing political palates Americans have. During
the presidential primary, the nation wanted to have hope in
a system that seemed to fail them. Could we believe that
there was a leader who cared about our concerns? Was
it unfair to want a leader that wouldn't put their polarizing,
partisan issues ahead of the welfare of things like having a
job that provides for our family or quality education systems
for our children?

Hillary Clinton was surely an adequate answer to those
questions, except people had already made up their minds
that the person who was a champion for causes, that supported endeavors like providing universal health care for
children, was nothing more than a bitch. The person that

supported family in a glaringly personal way on a national stage was just a bitch.

A part of her losing was because she had to compete with the parallels of her conceived image versus the picture of a strong, capable leader. Furthermore, her loss was predicated on the fact that her, along with other candidates', organization was based on a model that Obama's team made look archaic. They spent resources going after people that never participated in the political process, talked to them in their language, and held their hands through the entire process while encouraging them along the way that YES, WE CAN! Obama's organization created a new template for presenting a candidate to the nation. Their platform centered on a highly engaged electorate. They took people who were interested in their candidate and turned them into supporters then into friends and finally into family—so that, no matter what, they were going to support Obama. At times their support seemed so cultish that the world was looking for an excuse for the successfulness of their operation, when the answer all along was that they created a new platform to engage voters, one that they executed well enough to manifest a victory.

I, along with young, wet-behind-the-ears organizers, fought a good fight. We gave it our all. She lost, and though I long for the resurgence of Hillary Clinton, the field is now cleared for new contenders.

ABOUT THE AUTHOR

Amanda V. Wilkerson is an educator, community activist and political organizer dedicated to defining and exploring the pathology of African American civic engagement. Her work includes serving of the vice president and secretary of a local chapter of College Democrats, an inaugural board member of Campus Progress, director of Student Lobbying, Iowa field organizer for the Hillary Clinton Presidential Committee, African American outreach organizer for the Hillary Clinton Presidential Committee, advance team member for the Hillary Clinton Presidential Committee, field organizer for Florida for Obama, creator of Potluck and Politics and executive director of Activist in Action. Wilkerson teaches U.S. history at a local middle school in Kissimmee, Fla. This is her first book.

Visit:
amandawilkerson.org